Original title:
Slip 'N Slide: Winter Edition

Copyright © 2024 Creative Arts Management OÜ
All rights reserved.

Author: Beckett Sinclair
ISBN HARDBACK: 978-9916-94-280-2
ISBN PAPERBACK: 978-9916-94-281-9

Frosty Fables

In the snow, we glide and slip,
A frosty dance, a crazy trip.
With boots on wrong and laughter loud,
We tumble down, a snowy crowd.

The penguins cheer from icy sheets,
While snowmen laugh at our cold feats.
Marshmallow fluff flies through the air,
As we spin round without a care.

Hot cocoa waits for us inside,
To warm our hearts from winter's ride.
Yet here we are, in snowball fights,
Creating chaos, pure delight.

So grab your sled, let's race once more,
In this winter land we all adore.
With giggles echoing all around,
Frosty fables in joy abound.

Frosted Laughter

Snowflakes dance upon my nose,
Children giggle, laughter flows.
A tumble here, a fumble there,
Wiping snowballs from my hair.

Sleds zoom by with squeals and shouts,
Frosty air, a chill about.
We slip and slide, then down we go,
A snowman's hat? It's now a toe!

Frigid Funhouse

Wobbly boots and frozen toes,
Skating round like silly crows.
Ice-cream faces, rosy cheeks,
Laughter echoes, all it speaks.

A snowball flies, a friendly race,
I turn, I slide, oh, what a place!
A frosty slip, a funny fall,
We gather round, we laugh, we call.

Chilling Conquests

The hill is high, my heart beats loud,
With a whoosh, I'm flying proud.
A twist, a turn, hands in the air,
Laughter floats on winter's air.

We conquer slopes with squeaky glee,
A snowman battle, just you and me.
Frosty foes, we give our best,
In winter's kingdom, we jest and rest.

Glacial Adventure

A cartwheel made on frozen ground,
Laughter's echo is all around.
Falling flat, oh what a sight,
Like penguins dancing, pure delight.

Sliding past on glacial beams,
We slice through winter's frosty dreams.
With giggles loud and spirits high,
Together here, we laugh and fly.

Frosty Exhilaration

When winter sneaks in, watch your step,
A frosty surprise can cause quite a rep.
With laughter and squeals, we glide with flair,
A tumble, a roll, we just don't care!

Snowballs like missiles, they fly through the air,
Best dodge them all—some might be unfair!
Giddy giggles echo as we get cold,
Our icy adventures never grow old!

Glistening Iceways

On glistening paths where few dare to tread,
We race with bold hearts, but watch for the spread!
A slip and a slide, we start to unwind,
Grinning like kids, no worries in mind!

Penguins and polar bears are our cheer,
Who needs grades when we've got this here?
With bruised but proud bums, we leap frosty hills,
Chasing each other, igniting the thrills!

Shimmering Snow Trails

The shimmering snow gleams under the sun,
We shoot down the slopes—oh, what a run!
Hurdling over bumps, we let out a shriek,
As pillows of powder land on our cheeks!

Armies of snowmen march with great pride,
Our laughter erupts as we tumble and glide.
We build fortresses high, the cold we embrace,
With snowball assaults, we're setting the pace!

Whirlwind of White

In a whirlwind of white, we spin round in glee,
As winter wraps us in its icy decree.
With friends by our side, we conquer the fray,
Each tumble and trip just brightens the day!

Hot cocoa awaits, our reward at the end,
We share all the stories with each other's friend.
So here's to the moments that make us collide,
In frosty hijinks, there's joy to abide!

Snowbound Sprints

In a blizzard's embrace, we dash and dive,
A snowball fight starts, our laughter alive.
With cheeks all aglow and hats boldly askew,
We tumble and roll, like kids we once flew.

With each frosty breath, we giggle and cheer,
As snowflakes come down, we have nothing to fear.
In the chaos of cold, with friends by our side,
We race down the hill—let's take the wild ride!

Icy Playground

The swings creak and groan beneath coats piled high,
On frozen slides, we soar and we fly.
With mittens all soggy, and noses turned red,
We squeal as we tumble, our joy widespread.

In this frigid fairground, we twirl and we spin,
A cartwheel on ice? Oh, where to begin!
The pavement now slicker, we wobble with glee,
A comedy show, starring you and me!

Winter's Playful Glide

A sled at the ready, we gather in packs,
With giggles and grins, we launch for the tracks.
Like rockets we shoot, with arms flailing wide,
And land in a heap, snow angels our guide.

The frosty wind whistles, but we laugh it away,
With hot cocoa dreams of sweet, chocolaty play.
As we stumble and trip, this chill feels so nice,
Winter's a playground, so warm and so bright!

Frostbite Frolic

In a crunch of the snow, we leap and we bound,
With each hilarious fall, the cold wraps around.
Stumbling and slipping, we make quite a scene,
A ballet of winter, in jackets of green.

The laughter erupts as we plunge to the ground,
In snowflakes and giggles, pure joy can be found.
As we roll in the fluff, like puppies at play,
Winter's frisky charm makes us dance and sway!

Frozen Flights

In snowball fights, we take our aim,
With laughter loud, we play the game.
We slip and trip and lose our hats,
Like clumsy penguins, how we sat!

The icy patch becomes a stage,
As we perform, both bold and sage.
With arms outstretched, we start to glide,
Then tumble down, oh what a ride!

Sledding Serenade

Down the hill, we zoom and soar,
Our sleds go flying, what a roar!
With squeals of glee, we take the leap,
Into the snow, oh what a heap!

A snowman waits, his eyes will spy,
As we collide with quite a sigh.
Together we laugh, the day's delight,
As winter wraps us, snug and tight.

Snowdrift Circus

The circus comes to winter's land,
Where snowmen juggle, oh so grand.
With icy chills and frosty cheer,
The winter show brings all the gear!

On snowflakes high, we leap and twirl,
As glistening flakes around us whirl.
Each tumble brings a laugh out loud,
As snowflakes fall, oh so proud!

Crystal Cascades

In frosty fields where mischief plays,
We skate on ice in funny ways.
With every slide and every spin,
We find the giggles deep within!

The winter sun begins to shine,
Reflects on frost, a sparkling line.
With joyful hearts, we take a chance,
As laughter leads us in our dance!

Shimmering Slopes

On frosty days, we glide with glee,
With laughter loud, just you and me.
Snowflakes dance, a sparkling flight,
We navigate through pure delight.

Wobbly legs on icy ground,
A tumble here, a giggle found.
With every trip, a tale unfolds,
As friends together, brave and bold.

The hilly bumps, a thrilling rush,
In winter's chaos, we all blush.
Snowballs fly, friendships ignite,
In this cold wonderland, pure light.

With rosy cheeks and winter gear,
We conquer slopes without a fear.
Each slide down feels like a dream,
Icy laughter, a joyful scream.

Frozen Adventures

A vivid chill, the air is bright,
We gear up tight, chasing delight.
With sleds in hand, the race begins,
To see who falls and who just grins.

The snowballs fly, like cannonballs,
As laughter echoes through the halls.
We slip and slide, then take a fall,
In this frozen world, we have a ball.

With frosty noses and cheeky smiles,
Our joy stretches across the miles.
Every plunge and wiggle spree,
A chilly day, wild and free.

Even if we tumble down,
We trade our frowns for funny crowns.
In frozen fun, we take the lead,
Adventures here, we all can heed.

Arctic Sledding Tales

Down the hill we come with zest,
A sledding game, we're on a quest.
Through giggles bright, our spirits soar,
As we tumble down, wanting more.

Snowflakes twirl like dance routines,
We're kings and queens of winter scenes.
With every sled, a story grows,
Each epic fail, the fun just flows.

From snowy peaks to icy plains,
We share the laughter, dodge the trains.
Oh, that bump made quite a sound,
With clumsy grace, we hit the ground.

Through frosty air, our joy takes flight,
In this winter game, we hold so tight.
With sleds in hand, we make our way,
Each tale we share makes our day.

Chilling Chutes

The frosty air gives us the giggles,
We charge ahead, dodging the wiggles.
On chutes we slip, with speed to boast,
In this winter wonder, we laugh the most.

With cheeks aglow, we race like mad,
Every little fall, oh how we've had.
Snowflakes twinkle, laughter rings,
We bounce back up, oh, what joy it brings!

Tumbling down, we roll and play,
No frowns allowed on this bright day.
With every run, our hearts entwine,
Chilling chutes, oh how we shine!

These winter games, they bring such cheer,
In frozen realms, our fun is clear.
So grab your gear, it's time to glide,
In this chilly world, we take a ride.

Magical Winter Trails

In a park, we gather round,
Sleds and laughter, joy abounds.
Snowflakes swirl, a frosty dance,
Who will tumble? Who has a chance?

Hot cocoa warms our chilly hands,
As we slide on our winter bands.
The trees are draped in white delight,
We zip and zoom, what a silly sight!

I hear a shout, a kid takes flight,
Over wheels, what a funny plight!
With every glide, there's giggles loud,
Who knew snow could make us proud?

Snowballs flying, a comet's tail,
Oh! Look out, it's a snowball hail!
Laughing faces, cheeks all aglow,
We chase the fun, where no one goes!

Icy Joyrides

Watch us race on frosty tracks,
We spin and dip, no time to relax.
Snowmen waving as we fly by,
With every turn, we reach for the sky.

Winter's chill fills up the air,
But our laughter? Beyond compare!
Sleds collide, a comic crash,
Into a snowdrift, we make a splash!

Parents watch with eyes so wide,
While kids tumble down the slide.
Icy pathways, oh so slick,
Hilarity strikes, it's quite the trick!

In our kingdom of snowy cheer,
It's all about the fun, we fear!
With frozen grins from ear to ear,
Come join the joy, winter's near!

Glide of the Snowflakes

On a glittery winter's morn,
Snowflakes dance, laughter is born.
Tiny slips, oh, what a show,
Round and round, we twirl and go.

Warming hearts in chilly breeze,
Falling down with such great ease.
One more push, we take the leap,
Laughter rolling, oh so steep!

Chasing friends down snowy shawls,
Down we go, laughing with falls.
Over bumps, we scream and glide,
What a ride, come take the side!

The winter playground, full of fun,
Underneath the sparkling sun.
Frolicking, sliding, cheer on high,
Join the mischief, give it a try!

Winter Cascade Adventures

The hill's a mountain, made for play,
Let's race down, hip-hip-hooray!
With our sleds, we carve the ground,
Chuckle echoes all around.

Frosty faces, redness blooms,
Tumbling down, we dodge the glooms.
Laughter rings like silver bells,
We share the joy as winter dwells.

Oh dear! Someone's lost a hat,
Rolling down, imagine that!
We laugh and cheer in gleeful fun,
As snowballs fly, our games begun.

The sun dips low; we won't relent,
With frosty hearts, we're heaven-sent.
Adventurous slides and gleeful grins,
In winter's grasp, let the fun begin!

Glacial Grace

Fingers numb as snowballs fly,
A tumbling neighbor, oh my, oh my!
With laughter echoing, we plot and scheme,
The frozen pond becomes our dream.

Frosty hats sit askew, so grand,
As we glide forth, hand in hand.
Under skies a glistening hue,
Our ice skates say, "Look at you!"

Wipe out moments, pure delight,
As we crash under the pale moonlight.
In the frost, we lose all grace,
But find our joy in the race.

Snowmen wobble, hats askew,
Each tumble brings a giggle, too.
With each frosty spell we find,
Winter's laughter, intertwined.

Icicle Interludes

Hanging down like nature's spears,
Watch your head and cling to cheers!
Icicles dangling, glinting bright,
"Be careful!" echoes, pure delight.

In the backyard, a slide so slick,
"Last one down is a rotten stick!"
We race and tumble, whoosh and spin,
Grinning wide at our dizzy win.

Warmed by cocoa, tales unfold,
Of snowball fights — we're brave and bold.
Snowflakes drift with cheeky flair,
Our shouts of joy fill winter air.

Noses red, we gather round,
As frosty stories abound.
With every slide and snowy slip,
We raise our mugs and let it rip!

Sledding Secrets

The hill's a mountain, or so we say,
With sleds that glide, we're on our way.
Tucked in tight, we scream and yell,
As we plummet down, it's pure magic spell.

Hidden treasures in a snowdrift peek,
A melted snack or two we seek.
Tracking trails with frosty boots,
Sledding buddies, oh what hoots!

The sledding adventures, tales of old,
With every fall, more courage bold.
Armored in layers, we laugh till bright,
Falling faces make frosty bites!

Under the stars, we gather at last,
Recap the slopes from the frosty blast.
With cheeks a-glow, our laughter rings,
Winter secrets, oh, the joy it brings!

Frosty Frolics

Grab a scarf, it's time for fun,
Frosty frolics have begun!
With every leap and jibber jab,
We'll slide and glide like a magic lab.

Snowflakes twirl in a winter dance,
Watch that puddle—take a chance!
Face plants happen, style be dashed,
Yet our giggles are never trashed.

Racing down with cheeks aglow,
Falling faster, oh, what a show!
Behind us trails of laughter soar,
In this chill, we find our core.

Wrap it up beneath the stars,
Drinks in hand, we're winter's czars.
With every winter, tales will thrive,
For joy is where we come alive!

Frosty Footprints

Tiny tracks in the snow,
Must've been a little crow.
Mittens flapping in the breeze,
Chasing after frosty leaves.

Sleds go flying, kids all scream,
Giggling like it's just a dream.
But wait—what's that on the path?
A tumble brings a laugh and wrath!

Snowballs flying left and right,
Landing with a giggly bite.
One little slip and down I go,
A frosty face, a perfect show!

Winding Winter Trails

Winding trails of gleaming white,
Skates and sleds, what a sight!
Everyone's a graceful pro,
'Til they hit the ice and go!

Laughter echoes through the air,
As friends fly by without a care.
Here comes grandma, slipping fast,
Her wig flies off—oh what a blast!

Snowflakes dance like silly sprites,
In the glow of winter nights.
Twirling, spinning, what a whirl,
Belly flops and snow-filled curls!

Chill and Cheer

Gather 'round the frosty fire,
With hot cocoa—oh, desire!
Sipping slow, we take a pause,
While kids throw snow—what caused this clause?

A smidgen slip, a tumble round,
Who knew winter's glee could astound?
With every laugh, a chimney smoke,
In this chill, we're just plain broke!

Snowflakes fall like silly seeds,
After laughter, everyone bleeds.
Wipe your face, the cold will bite,
But we rise up with sheer delight!

Winter's Wet Whimsy

Wet and wild, the snowflakes spin,
Creating laughter from within.
Watch the puppy leap with glee,
Chasing rabbits, oh so free!

Soggy mittens on the ground,
Children tumbling all around.
In the chaos, spins a friend,
Lands in snow—hey, let's pretend!

Splashing snow beneath our feet,
With every jump, the joy's complete.
Through the drifts, we dance and slide,
In winter's hug, we'll glide and ride!

Snowbound Slaloms

In snowdrifts deep, we take our chance,
With sleds in hand, it's time to dance.
We zig and zag, the laughter flies,
As snowflakes tumble from the skies.

A twisty turn, we scream with glee,
My friend forgot to steer, oh me!
We crash and roll, a frosty pile,
Emerging grinning, snowman style.

With cocoa mugs and rosy cheeks,
We share our tales for days and weeks.
The snowball fights in twilight glow,
Who'd guess we'd slip, or how we'd throw?

So grab your gear, don't miss the fun,
The icy hills we've just begun!
With winter's charm, we slide and glide,
Embrace the joy—let's take that ride!

Frigid Rides

A toboggan waits, let's take a spin,
The frostbit rhythm, let's begin!
With frosty breaths, we brave the chill,
As laughter echoes down the hill.

In winter's gleam, we zoom and soar,
With cheeks like apples, we crave for more.
But whoops! A tumble, and down we go,
In tangled limbs and heaps of snow.

A wobbly drift, we steer askew,
Oh, someone's snack just blew right through!
Cookies fly and flurries swirl,
We're a winter scene, a merry whirl!

So gather round, let the stories fly,
Of frigid rides and snowflakes high.
With every cheer, the cold's alright,
In winter's wild and magical light!

Winter's Waterfall

The slopes are steep, a thrilling sight,
Our hearts race fast, we're feeling light.
With one big push, we sail and scream,
Down icy slopes like a winter dream!

But wait! We hit a bump too soon,
A launch so high, we kiss the moon!
Through frosty air, we start to glide,
Then tumble down the frosty slide.

We plow through banks like rolling snowmen,
In fits of laughter, we try again.
The chill surrounds, but joy ignites,
This cascade of laughs on winter nights.

Hold on tight, the fun won't stop,
As friends unite with every plop.
We swear one day we'll learn to steer,
Until then, let's all cheer, my dear!

Crystal Creekings

Through glistening paths, we run and race,
With icy smiles, we find our place.
In winter's realm, we tease and glide,
Down crystal creekings, side by side.

Oh, watch out now! A hidden bump,
Squeals of joy—a mighty thump!
With flying limbs and shocked delight,
We land like snowflakes, soft and light.

A slippery bridge, a daring leap,
In bursts of giggles, we barely keep.
But as we slip, we don't mind,
It's all in fun, our joys combined.

So gather 'round at winter's call,
Let's make some memories, one and all.
Through frosty trails and laughter bright,
We'll cherish these days, oh what a sight!

The Frosty Odyssey

Frostbite nipped my nose, oh dear,
I slipped and fell, but had no fear.
Snowflakes twirled, a dance so bright,
Laughter echoed, pure delight.

A penguin slid right past my face,
Wobbling around, what a funny race!
I grabbed my sled, went down the hill,
Laughing so hard, I lost all skill.

Friends rolling snowballs, a snowball fight,
Whizzing by me, oh what a sight!
"Duck!" I yelled, but it was too late,
Face full of snow, such a funny fate.

From snowmen built to winter's games,
We're all just kids calling each other names.
In the frosty air, giggles collide,
What a wild and wondrous ride!

Winter's Hidden Slides

In the park, we laugh and glide,
On hidden paths, we slide with pride.
Chilly winds can't stop our spree,
With cheeks so red, we're wild and free.

The hill looks steep, but watch us go,
Screaming in laughter, then "Oh no!"
Cartwheeling down like snowflakes spun,
Each twist and turn, we're having fun.

A snowman waves with a carrot nose,
Under the tree, a snowball throws.
"Catch me if you can!" someone shouts,
As the winter joy erupts in shouts.

Falling over, it's a snowy mess,
Still we rise up, never less.
With spirits high and laughter wide,
As winter's magic makes us glide.

Echoes of Winter Fun

Echoes of laughter fill the air,
As we tumble down without a care.
Snowflakes land on our noses' tips,
The chilly thrill makes our laughter flip.

Winter's call brings all our crew,
To slide with glee in a frosty hue.
Sleds in tow, we race the sun,
"Ready, set, go!" Here comes the fun!

Mittens fly and scarves take flight,
We spin and twirl in pure delight.
The snowball fight, a comical cheer,
With every throw, we jump in sheer.

Snow angels made with arms out wide,
The joy of winter, we cannot hide.
In this frozen wonderland, we play,
Creating memories that forever stay.

Chill-tastic Adventures

Rolling down hills, we can't resist,
Winter fun, wrapped in a mist.
With friends by our side and laughter loud,
We take on winter, daring and proud.

Snowflakes landing, like giggles fall,
In this frosty kingdom, we have a ball.
An icy patch is now our stage,
As we slip and slide, the fun's the gauge.

A snowball flurry, a cheeky strike,
"Run for cover!" Oh, what a hike!
Chasing each other, we dance and glide,
In this winter wonder, we take great pride.

As the day ends, we build a fort,
Stuck in laughter, for fun we've sought.
These chill-tastic adventures so grand,
In this winter wonderland, hand in hand.

Icicle Escapade

One frosty morn, down the hill I go,
With a boot on my foot, and a hat on my toe.
I stumble and tumble, oh what a sight,
Like a fish out of water, in glorious flight.

Neighbors all gather, they can't help but stare,
As I roll and I slide, with frosty hair.
"That's not how to glide!" they cheer from afar,
While I wave my arms, the ice is bizarre.

My sled's gone rogue, on its own little spree,
It's darting away, way too fast for me.
With laughter erupting, I flail like a seal,
Guess winter's charm is how I feel.

So come join the ruckus, the snow's a delight,
Sledding and sliding till day turns to night.
Embrace the mayhem, let joy be your guide,
In this frosty circus, there's nothing to hide.

Winter's Whirl

In a flurry of flakes, kids spin with glee,
Chasing each other, as wild as can be.
A snowball takes flight, oh, watch where you duck,
As everyone giggles, good luck if you're stuck!

They build a grand snowman, a creature so proud,
With a carrot for a nose, he's laughing out loud.
Then down goes a friend, face-planted in snow,
While the rest of us laugh, what a comical show!

A snowman brigade, they stumble and sway,
As the wind starts to howl, they dance in dismay.
"A hat's not a shield!" someone shouts in despair,
But the wintery chaos fills all with good cheer.

So gather around, let the fun times ignite,
In the fabulous frolic of frosty delight.
With snowflakes a-flying and joy all around,
We conquer the chill, with laughter abound.

Glide Through the Chill

Whee! Off I go, on a sled made of dreams,
With a wobbly start, or so it seems.
Hitting a bump, I soar like a kite,
Lands with a thud, oh what a weird flight!

My mittens are soaked, with splashes galore,
As I flounder and fumble, I can't take much more.
But wait! Here comes Buddy, a pro on the steed,
Flying down the slope, he's the one I need!

A charm of the winter pulls all who adore,
The antics of slipping—or sliding—once more.
Each tumble and trip, a highlight of bliss,
In this race of the snow, it's laughter we miss!

So join in the madness, on ice like a pro,
Where fun reigns supreme, and no one is slow.
With cheeks red as cherries, and breath chilly white,
In this wintery wonder, everything feels right.

Snow Whisper Journeys

Under a pale sky, we march to the drift,
Where the flavor of winter gives each sled a lift.
Whispers of snowflakes, soft as a dream,
As we careen forward, giggling the theme.

A grand snowball duel starts right on the road,
Dodging each other, our coolness bestowed.
But wait—who's that? A wild puppy's surprise,
He leaps in the fray with mischief in his eyes!

Zooming on gliders, my heart's in a whirl,
As I spin in a flurry, my hair starts to twirl.
With frosty winds blowing, we're champions of fun,
Taking tumbling turns 'til the day is done.

With memories crafted in a flurry and cheer,
We'll laugh at the stories that winter holds dear.
So let's take the plunge into this snowy shindig,
For the joy that it brings, oh, let's dance a jig!

Icy Ventures

On a hill of glistening white,
Racing friends in sheer delight,
Snowballs fly with laughter loud,
Chasing giggles, feeling proud.

Sleds go bump, a crazy ride,
Sliding fast, we dare the tide,
Frosty air, what fun it brings,
Winter's joy in silly flings.

Wipeouts happen, we can't resist,
Snowy faces, hands and fists,
Rolling down, a frosty fall,
Hilarity in the winter squall.

Hot cocoa waits, with marshmallow cheer,
We'll toast to fun, with friends so near,
Snowy antics won't fade away,
In these icy ventures, we'll always play.

Nippy Nonsense

Winter's chill is here to stay,
Watch us tumble, hip hooray!
Gloves and scarves, what a mess,
Slipping past, we just confess.

Frosty air, our cheeks aglow,
Whirl and twirl, we steal the show,
Chasing snowflakes mid-flight,
Making merry till the night.

Upside down, our hats askew,
Snowman's smile is just for you,
Rounding corners, we collide,
Silly joy that cannot hide.

Chattering teeth, laughter bright,
In this frosty, wild delight,
With each slip, we find our groove,
Nippy nonsense, we just move.

Flakes of Joy

Falling snow, a feather touch,
Giggles spark, we love it much,
Chasing flakes, each tiny piece,
In this season, our hearts increase.

Slipping here, we shout oh no,
Twirling like a dancing snow,
Brushing off the icy ground,
Finding joy where laughs are found.

Snowmen grinning, bright and round,
In this winter, fun abounds,
Frosty fingers, rosy cheeks,
This is where the laughter peaks.

So let's frolic, chase and glide,
In our coats we snuggly hide,
Flakes of joy, we laugh and play,
In a wonderland, hip-hip-hooray!

Joyous Winter Slides

Sleigh bells ringing, down we zoom,
In the snow, we chase our gloom,
Laughter echoing through the trees,
Winter's magic warms the freeze.

Friends go flying, squeals of glee,
Hats all sideways, can't you see?
Slippery paths with tales to tell,
In these slides, we know so well.

Snowball fights and quick retreats,
Chilly cheeks and frosty feats,
Words of wisdom shared in fun,
Joyous winter has just begun.

Through the flakes, we share our glee,
Every slide a victory,
Hot cocoa waits at winter's end,
For these moments, we will bend.

Slippery Revelries

Frosty paths and hidden drops,
We glide and tumble, laughter flops.
Snowy socks and mismatched shoes,
Winter brings us funny blues.

Down we slide, oh what a ride,
Gravity's game, we cannot hide.
With every fall, a joyful shout,
Winter fun, that's what it's about.

Snowballs fly, with playful aim,
Who needs sleds? We've got our game.
A spin, a twist, on frosty lands,
Our winter sport, all unplanned.

So grab a friend, let's take a chance,
On icy paths, we laugh and prance.
With every slip, we find delight,
In winter's joy, we ignite the night.

Cold Currents

Here we bounce, on glassy glides,
Chasing snowflakes, joy abides.
Wobbling hearts and chilly cheeks,
What's next, oh, the thrill it seeks!

Pants are wet, and giggles soar,
A frosty tumble, we want more.
Snowmen frown at our wild ride,
Yet we bask in merry pride.

Winter winds play tricks so sly,
As we zoom, and slip, and fly.
A hop, a skip, we lose our feet,
Blissful chaos, pure and sweet.

We'll dance with glee, till sunset's glow,
In this winter, laughter flows.
So join the fun, take off the frowns,
With every slide, we lose our crowns.

The Joy of Slipping

On frozen paths, we take our chance,
A stumble here, a snowy dance.
Boots are slick, we laugh and trip,
Each little fall, a happy blip.

Cocoa cheers, and rosy cheeks,
Perfect moments in our peaks.
Winter whispers funny tales,
While laughter scales the snowy trails.

Falling down, oh what a sight,
As the world spins day to night.
A twist, a turn, we break the mold,
The joy of slipping never gets old.

So come along, embrace the cheer,
For winter's gifts are always near.
With every glide, we find our muse,
In joyful slips, we cannot lose.

Winter Wonderland Waltz

In the waltz of icy grace,
We twirl and spin, what a race!
Snowflakes tickle, cold and bright,
As we slip through the gentle night.

With giggles loud, we steal the show,
Twirling friends, in the white glow.
A slide to the left, a dip to the right,
Our winter ball, a pure delight.

Under stars, oh, what a scene,
Chasing dreams where we've been.
Each fumble brings us laughter warm,
In this dance, we dare the storm.

Mittens fly, as we glide along,
With winter's rhythm, we sing our song.
So come take part in our snowy jest,
In this winter waltz, we are truly blessed.

Frosty Flights of Fancy

In snowy gear, we take our flight,
Wobbling forth, what a delight!
With laughter loud, we lose our grace,
As frozen cheeks beam a silly face.

A flying flop, then off we go,
Down the hill, what a wild show!
With arms and legs all in a tangle,
Our frozen thrills — oh, how they dangle!

Icicles dangle from winter's art,
As we tumble, it's a la carte!
With sleds and laughter, the fun won't end,
A slippery journey with every bend.

So grab a friend, let's race and slide,
Through drifts and hills, with laughter as our guide!
Together we roll, in chaotic bliss,
Frosty flights, oh, how can we miss?

Chilled Cheer

Hot cocoa spills on my cozy lap,
As we dash outside for a frosty nap.
Snowflakes swirl, a winter ballet,
While we frolic and tumble, come what may.

Squeaky boots as we dash around,
Making snowmen, we're glory-bound!
But oops! A miss, down goes a hat,
Laughter erupts — oh, how about that?

A snowball flies, aiming for me,
Dodging and giggling beneath the tree.
The chilly air is filled with cheer,
Wipe that snow off, let's engineer!

Winter play, what a splendid show,
Waltzing with snowflakes — don't be slow!
Together we shine, the sun peeks through,
Chilled cheer we make, just me and you!

Serene Slopes

Up the hill, it's a peaceful climb,
With joyous hearts, we beat the time.
A lofty perch, the world below,
In quiet moments, we steal the show.

But wait! A tumble, down we go,
What a sight, this winter tableau!
With grace we lose, and giggles rise,
As powder poofs up to the skies.

It's serene here, till chaos reigns,
Amidst the weaves and frosty chains.
Together we sway, it's a raucous dream,
Down the slopes, we laugh and scream.

As silence beckons, a moment divine,
But laughter soon breaks, it draws the line.
In serene slopes, where joy abides,
It's a winter wonder where fun collides!

Winter's Euphoria

In flurries light, we twist and spin,
Chasing each other, let the fun begin!
With rosy cheeks and eyes so bright,
A gleeful dance in the snowy white.

With each playful hop, a giggle escapes,
Snowball battles, where fun reshapes.
We build a fortress, pat with glee,
In our winter kingdom, wild and free.

A charm of laughter fills the air,
As mischief weaves with frosty flair.
Slipping a bit, we tumble and roll,
Euphoria hugs us, warming our soul.

So here we are, in this winter's grip,
Holding tight to every crazy trip.
With joyous hearts, we cannot hide,
In this season's glow, we take that ride!

Frosty Escapades

In a jacket two sizes too big,
I venture out with a jig.
The snow greets me with a squeak,
As I trip and land with a peak.

Laughter spills from my friends nearby,
As I tumble in a snowball fly.
With cheeks rosy and spirits high,
It's clear winter's the reason why!

A snowman shimmies, so chubby and round,
While I chase my sled down without a sound.
With a whoosh and a giggle, we race through the air,
Oh, the frosty fun—we haven't a care!

So here's to the laughter and winter's sweet chill,
To snowflakes and blunders, let's capture the thrill!
With every odd tumble, we spread winter cheer,
In this frosty wonder, there's nothing to fear!

The Art of Gliding

On a hilltop we gather, gleefully bold,
With sleds in our hands and laughter to hold.
Count three and we're off, it's a sight to behold,
Falling together makes a story retold.

The graceful arc of a tumbling slip,
Gives way to the joy of a clumsy trip.
Spinning in snow, just like a mad whip,
Who knew winter could be such a trip?

A penguin dance as we try to regain,
Our balance while laughing, dodging the pain.
With snowy delights and giggles as our chain,
We rewrite the rules on this frosty terrain.

The art of the glide is uniquely absurd,
A blend of pure joy, where laughter's preferred.
With snowflakes a-flying and spirits undeterred,
This winter affair is truly deferred!

The Chill of Delight

We bundle up tight, ready to play,
But the cold makes us shiver and sway.
Down the slope, we take flight,
Chilled to the bone, but what a delight!

Frost-bite giggles as we tumble and roll,
Each fall is a marvel, it takes quite a toll.
The chill in the air, it embraces our soul,
With snow in our hair, we are on a stroll.

Hot cocoa waits, a warm little treat,
But we race to the hill, for laughter's the beat.
Together we slip, in a dance oh-so sweet,
In this winter wonder, we can't know defeat!

So frost-covered cheeks and snorts of delight,
Unleashing the giggles under soft twilight.
In the dance of cold snow, adventures ignite,
The sheer joy it brings is truly out of sight!

Glory of the Glide

With a mighty push, we conquer the slope,
Our hearts filled with joy, our minds full of hope.
Each graceful descent, with laughter we cope,
Through chaos we fly, like a slippery rope.

A salute to the air as we teeter and twist,
With tumbling giggles not one to resist.
Landing face-first in snow, oh how we missed,
The elegance soaring—it's a frostbitten tryst.

From sleds to snowballs, our antics unfold,
A ballet in white, a frosty tale told.
We stumble and tumble, we're brave, we're bold,
With memories forming that never get old.

So here's to the winter, the laughter it seeds,
To playful adventures and whimsical deeds.
In the glory of gliding, our friendships exceed,
In this snowy ballet, our hearts are freed!

Icy Echoes

The ground is slick, a frosty show,
'Twas a daring leap, now I'm down low.
With laughter shared, we tumble and glide,
My backside's frosty from this wild ride.

We twirl and spin, like wacky seals,
A chorus of giggles, oh, how it feels!
Ice beneath us, we dance with glee,
Who knew that winter could set us free?

Snowflakes fly, we throw them high,
Like little missiles aiming for the sky.
But oh, the twist when we lose control,
It's a winter game that fills the soul!

So bring your boots, your hats, your cheer,
Join in the fun, there's nothing to fear!
With frosty breaths and wheezy grins,
This wintry escapade is where it begins.

Glistening Paths

The path is shining, a crystal maze,
My feet take off in a wild craze.
I wobble left, then veer right,
Oh, gravity wins this frosty fight!

A merry dance in the icy air,
As snowflakes land without a care.
A tumble here, a stumble there,
With frozen giggles that we all share.

We bumble and roll, in ditches we fall,
Yet laughter harmonizes, it trumps it all.
With icy cheeks and spirits bright,
We conquer the cold, a silly sight!

So grab your pals and join the spree,
Navigate this glistening sea.
For when we trip, we rise with glee,
Winter shenanigans, come join me!

Winter's Whirligig

Round and round on the icy floor,
We're tumbles and turns, then tumble some more.
Snowball fights lead to silly glee,
As we whirl away, just you and me.

With frosty mittens and scarves so bright,
We giggle and spin into the night.
The world's a blur of white and blue,
As frosty fun is all we pursue.

The wind, it howls, but we don't mind,
In our whirlpool of joy, blissfully blind.
We'll slip and slide till the night is done,
No treasure compares to this frozen fun.

So come join me in this circling spree,
Where laughter echoes, wild and free.
For in every spin, there's magic found,
In winter's embrace, our joy knows no bound!

Snowy Serpentines

The serpentines twist, like a dance on ice,
With each little wobble, it's perilous and nice.
We twist and we turn, with laughter so loud,
As we fly through the flakes that weaves our shroud.

Our feet take flight on this frosted course,
With giggles and grins, we feel the force.
A bump, then a roll, oh, what a sight,
Who knew winter could bring this delight?

With snow in our hair and joy in our hearts,
We dart and we dash, playing our parts.
No worries about falling or making a splash,
Just winter's charm and a spontaneous dash!

So join in the fun on these snowy ways,
Where every tumble sparks endless praise.
In this vivid whirl, where we laugh and glide,
Winter's magic keeps our spirits wide!

Frosty Thrills

In the icy park, we take a chance,
With laughter loud, we start our dance.
A jovial slip, then down we go,
Landing in snow, wrapped in white glow.

Snowballs fly, our cheeks go red,
A giggling troop, we bounce instead.
With frosty breath, we race anew,
Who'll drift the farthest? A winter zoo!

Mittens stuck to our frozen cheeks,
Silly faces, it's fun we seek.
Wobbling like penguins, oh what a sight,
Chasing our friends in pure delight.

Hot cocoa waits, with marshmallows big,
To warm our hearts from dancing a jig.
As we recount, our frosty spills,
It's just good fun, these frosty thrills.

Chilling Cascades

Down the hill, we tumble and roll,
A frosty river, takes its toll.
With legs in the air, and heads upside down,
We laugh so hard, we're the kings of the town.

A snowman waits with a scarf of bright cheer,
But first, we zoom past, shouting, "Look here!"
The sleds go crashing, a comical show,
Slide right into, a pile of snow.

With cheeks aglow, we'll take a wild ride,
Waving at friends as we slip and glide.
Bumping and giggling, what a messy spree,
Winter's the time for a frosty jubilee!

We race to the bottom, oh what a thrill,
Spinning and tumbling, we can't keep still.
Gathering laughter, in each other's gaze,
Chilling cascades, in frosty sun rays.

Glacial Glides

With sleds in tow, we gather our crew,
Ready for fun, with a clear sky so blue.
Racing like pro's, in this glacial zone,
Misty breath puffs as we skate on our own.

Like clowns on ice, we wobble and sway,
Each glide brings giggles, come join the play!
We're slipping away in a flurry of white,
Oops! There goes Tim, what a comical sight!

Snowflakes whirl as we fly down the hill,
Trips and tumbles, an absolute thrill.
No worries at all, it's laughter we seek,
In this frosty world, we're feeling unique.

At last, we gather under moon's glow,
Relishing moments of laughter in tow.
With hearts light as snow, we shout in delight,
These glacial glides, oh what a night!

Frost-Flecked Journeys

Suit up in layers, we gear up with glee,
A frosty adventure awaits you and me.
Shuffling and sliding, we hop on our rides,
With chilly winds laughing, as joy kindly bides.

Snow angels ready, we take to the ground,
With arms spread wide, in a flurry we're found.
Each frosty flake that settles with grace,
Brings back our giggles, a wintry embrace.

A misstep here, and a tumble there too,
We're rolling and laughing, oh what a view!
Wielding our sleds like mighty brave knights,
Chasing our shadows in frosty moonlight.

With cocoa in hand, we share tales tonight,
Of epic slides, and laughter so bright.
These frost-flecked journeys, we cherish and cheer,
In winter's embrace, we hold our friends dear.

Cold Dance

Snowflakes twirl in the air,
Kids are sliding without a care.
Laughter echoes, giggles soar,
Winter's here, who could ask for more?

With frostbite toes, they laugh and squeal,
Landing hard, their spins reveal.
A snowman's made with arms akimbo,
They stumble by like a funny limbo.

Gloves are wet, they slip and slide,
'Til icy patches claim their pride.
But scrapes and bruises, oh what fun,
A winter dance has just begun!

Hot cocoa waits 'round the fire,
With marshmallows stacked a bit higher.
After the giggles, there lies the treat,
A cozy end to the chilly beat.

Joy in the Frost

Frosty mornings, the world aglow,
A playground made of ice and snow.
With boots laced tight, they rush on by,
Just a twist and a tumble—oh my!

Snowballs fly like little bombs,
Landing on heads and causing qualms.
Cackles erupt, a snowy spree,
Chasing friends, as wild as can be.

Sleds zoom down a glittery hill,
A rush of wind and a jolt of thrill.
But wooden planks can catch a soul,
A belly flop, pure winter goal!

With rosy cheeks, they gather round,
In snowman armies, silliness found.
Winter's joy in every frosty breath,
A dance with snowflakes, no thought of rest.

Crystal Gleam Run

In the glimmer of morning light,
Children race with pure delight.
Snow is sparkling, a brilliant sight,
Off they go, like stars in flight.

Stylish falls and silly flops,
They twirl and laugh, no need for stops.
Ice skates scratch, with wobbly flair,
Spinning around, they grasp the air.

A race to the hill, hearts beat fast,
Who will win? They're having a blast!
A leap of faith, then whoosh down they go,
In a frosty whirlwind, putting on a show.

Crystals glisten, a magic glow,
With winter giggles, the fun won't slow.
Hot soup awaits after the fun,
In this mighty chill, they're never done!

Adventures in Snow

Bundled up, they roam so free,
Building castles, just wait and see!
A friendly penguin's built with flair,
Little arms outstretched in the air.

Sleds flying down at lightning speed,
"Catch me if you can!" A joyful creed.
One tumbles in, snow flies around,
Laughter rumbles, a joyful sound.

Ball fights break out on every side,
As snowballs collide, they run to hide.
The chase is on, through trees they dart,
With every tumble, they steal each heart.

Soon it's time to head back home,
With rosy cheeks and hearts that roam.
Wishing for more of this wintry bliss,
Adventures in snow—they won't miss!

Sleet and Play

In the park with a grin,
Snowflakes dance on my chin.
A tumble here, a bobble there,
Winter's frolic, a snowy fair.

With socks on the slide, we take a plunge,
The chill in the air feels like a grunge.
Laughter erupts with each little fall,
Snowy hijinks, we can't get enough at all.

A hat flies off, the gloves are lost,
But who cares about the cost?
In this winter wonderland parade,
We'll keep on playing, excitement won't fade.

Cocoa waits as we make our way,
To warm our toes at the end of the day.
Sleet and play, what a treat,
Winter fun can't be beat!

The Great Ice Escape

On a frozen lake, we dare to glide,
With squeaky shoes and smiles wide.
We spin in circles, chasing our fate,
All while hoping we won't be late!

A comical crash, I giggle and yell,
Down goes a friend with a clumsy swell.
They slide in style, like a penguin parade,
With flailing arms, they just can't evade.

The boots we wore feel a bit too tight,
As we frolic and tumble in sheer delight.
From banks to slopes, we run and race,
Each little stumble is a funny embrace.

As the sun dips low, we gather 'round,
Tales of our antics, in laughter we're bound.
The Great Ice Escape, a glorious day,
Who knew winter fun could be this way?

Slides of Snowy Mystique

A secret hill, where giggles dwell,
We dash on down, oh what the hell!
A flurry of white, a tumble and roll,
Slides of snowy mystique take hold of our soul.

In the chaos of snowballs and shouts,
We dodge and weave, we jump and scout.
With splat! and a crack! someone went flying,
Into the drift, and oh, they're still trying!

Under the trees, we form a grand team,
A castle of snow, our frosty dream.
But watch out now! Here comes a sled,
Its speed defies reason; someone's gone red.

But as the day fades, beneath a pink sky,
We laugh at our antics, oh my, oh my!
In the land of slides, our worries disappear,
Just young hearts in winter, with nothing to fear.

Chilly Chaser

In a mitten chase, we run and glide,
Through the snow, we gleefully bide.
A friend behind me with a shriek and a laugh,
Trying to catch up; it's quite the gaff!

We take a sharp turn, the snow flies high,
Summer's past, but winter's a spy.
Face full of snow, I'm left in a daze,
Through trails of laughter, we stumble and sway.

Hot cocoa calls, but first, a big race,
With snowmen and trees, no time to waste.
Oops! There's a bump! Down with a thud,
In a pile of flurries, there's no time for blood!

As we shake off the snow and brush off our pride,
The chilly chaser's filled with merry ride.
With frozen toes and hearts oh so bright,
These winter capers are pure delight!

Rushing Through the Snow

In frosty boots we dash and dart,
With snowballs flying, it's a snow-filled art.
Laughter echoes, spirits soar,
As we tumble, roll, and ask for more.

The sleds come cruising, oh what a sight,
Bumps and giggles paint the night.
With every spill and splash we cheer,
A snowy chaos that brings us near.

Parents watch, their eyes go wide,
As kids create a snowy slide.
With every leap and twist we make,
We're bound to start a frosty quake!

So let's embrace this winter's glee,
A joyous ride for you and me.
Forget the chill, just come and play,
In this snowy wonderland today!

Serene Slides

Graceful descents on blankets white,
With laughter sparkling, pure delight.
Tummies sliding, arms outstretched,
Each little stumble is nicely etched.

Snowflakes swirl like dancing sprites,
Making herds and forts at nights.
While cheeks are rosy, spirits high,
We glide beneath the starry sky.

A gentle race, who can go fast?
But laughter wins, it's a blast!
Mom's hot cocoa waiting inside,
But first, a joyful, frosty ride!

Let's savor moments full of cheer,
In winter's magic, we persevere.
With every giggle, we defy the cold,
Building memories, bright and bold!

Frosty Escapades

With hats askew and scarves that sway,
We charge the hills, let's shout hooray!
Falling over, we squeal and laugh,
Creating magic on our frosty path.

The crunch of snow beneath our feet,
In this winter wonderland, oh so sweet.
Snowmen wobble, their noses bright,
As we dive into fun, pure delight.

Cheeks ablaze and fingers numb,
It's snowball wars, here they come!
A friendly battle, we laugh and flee,
In this frozen land, wild and free.

So join us now, the chill's alright,
With every tumble, we take flight.
As laughter lingers, and snowflakes fall,
Let's live the joy of winter's call!

Whispers of Chill

Whispers of chill dance in the air,
As hats fly high, without a care.
Giggles echo, sounds of play,
On this chilly, delight-filled day.

Sleds go flying, a comet's blaze,
Who can zip the longest gaze?
With every bounce and woosh we share,
In frosty fun, we find our flair.

Behind every snowdrift lies a friend,
In snowy mischief, joy won't end.
With cheeks aglow, we race and glide,
Towards winter magic, hearts open wide.

Hold tight to laughter, come join the spree,
Let's melt the chill, just you and me.
In snowy wonder, let's laugh aloud,
In the frosty fun, let's be proud!

Frost's Gentle Embrace

In a blanket of white, we take our chance,
With mittens and hats, we giggle and prance.
The snowflakes tickle our noses so bright,
We tumble and tumble, oh what a sight!

Our cheeks are all rosy, we roll like a ball,
Down the hill we go, laughing through it all.
With shouts of glee that echo around,
We embrace the frost, winter's joy found!

Hot cocoa awaits when the fun's all through,
With marshmallows floating like snowflakes, too.
We dream of adventures, the laughter we shared,
In frost's gentle arms, we know we are cared.

Our frosty escapades will always remain,
In the heart of winter, there's joy not in vain.
With every cold breath, and each frosty cheer,
Frost's gentle embrace keeps our spirits near.

Cool Breezes and Chilling Thrills

Oh what fun it is to slide on the ground,
With each chilly rush, we squeal and rebound.
Snowmen are grinning, their noses so bright,
As we zoom past them, what a silly sight!

The air crisp and clear, a frosty delight,
Our laughter spills out under moon's gleaming light.
A friendly snowball, aimed right at my head,
Now I'm on the ground, laughter's easily bred!

With scarves swirling round, like a dervish we spin,
Chasing the cold, let the mischief begin.
A slip or a slide, we're all in the race,
With smiles and giggles, this winter we embrace!

Snowflakes like confetti, they fall all around,
With each crash and bump, joy is what we've found.
Cool breezes blow through, yet we laugh without fear,
These chilling thrills make winter the best time of year!

Powdered Paths

A path made of powder, we venture with glee,
With sleds and with courage, oh just wait and see!
We blast down the slope, like bullets we fly,
Giggles explode, oh my, oh my!

Frosty breath curls in the nippy black air,
As I wipe off the snow from my nose in despair.
But a friend throws a snowball, it hits with a splat,
Now laughter erupts, I'll get you for that!

Falling like leaves in this frosty ballet,
We tumble and roll in a whimsical way.
With cheeks flushed like apples, and spirits so bold,
We paint winter's canvas with stories untold!

Adventures await on those powdered paths,
As joy sparkles bright in our goofy outlaughs.
In winter's embrace, come join in the fun,
For every wild moment is slip-sliding run!

Winter's Twinkle

Stars wink above in the crisp frosty night,
While kids deck the snow, oh what a sight!
In laughter we twirl, like flakes in the air,
With the joy and delight, there's magic to share!

Snowflakes are falling, our whims take to flight,
We leap and we dance in the soft glowing light.
A game of freeze tag on the white snowy floor,
Being tagged is a giggle, we shout out for more!

Chasing after friends, with frosty breath vain,
A frolic in winter, heaped high with pure fun.
The joy we create in the chilly night air,
With hearts full of laughter, the snow is our share!

Winter's twinkle glistens as we play and we glide,
In the beauty of moments, our spirit can't hide.
Beneath the moon's glow, our laughter will cling,
For in the shimmery snow, we all are the kings!

Ethereal Slides

In frosty gear we gather round,
To launch ourselves without a sound.
A gentle push, then whoosh we go,
As laughter echoes through the snow.

The ground is slick, a polished place,
With cheeks aglow, we pick up pace.
A tumble here, a tumble there,
We ride the winter's frosty flair.

Hot cocoa waits at journey's end,
With marshmallows to warmly blend.
So let's embrace this frigid cheer,
With every slide, we shed our fear.

With every gust, we dance with glee,
As snowflakes twirl, oh can't you see?
We laugh so hard, we start to cry,
Then back again, we rush and fly.

Powdered Pathways

Waddling forth in puffy suits,
Like awkward penguins in our boots.
A snowy bump, a squeaky slide,
We shimmy down the gleeful ride.

The world is white, a whimsical dream,
We chase each other, hear our scream.
A pile of snow, a perfect throne,
Until we fall, and fates are blown.

Sideways flops and giggling fits,
We toss the snow, oh what a hit!
In frosty hair, the sparkle shines,
Each joyful crash, like summer vines.

So grab your friends and take the leap,
In silly slides, we laugh and squeak.
From dusk to dawn, we'll joyfully glide,
Through powdered pathways, side by side.

Gales and Glides

With wind at back, we race the sun,
A wild ride, oh what a run!
Twists and turns, a spin in space,
Our flailing arms, a funny chase.

A gust of air sends us a-flying,
With comedic flair, weare not denying.
A sideways crash, we land in fame,
In snowy drifts, we'll stake our claim.

Two friends collide, a flurry of glee,
In frosty bursts, we're wild and free.
With noses red, we smile so wide,
In every gale, we take a ride.

From slushy dips to snowy climbs,
Our laughter rings, a song of whims.
With gales and glides, we take our chance,
And in this mess, we dare to dance.

Snowy Spirals

Round and round on a frosty curl,
Spinning 'round like a boy or girl.
A joyful trip beneath the trees,
With winter's breath, we swirl with ease.

Hats fly off; they sail away,
In snowy spells, we laugh and play.
A winter wonder, oh what a scene,
With every turn, we feel like queens.

Each spiraled path a comical ride,
The world a blur as we glide.
Snowflakes dance in the glowing light,
In goofy spins, our hearts take flight.

So twirl and spin, embrace the chill,
With crazy trails, we find our thrill.
With snowy spirals, let us unite,
In laughter's joy, through day and night.

Icy Whirls

In frosty boots, we take our stance,
A wild adventure, oh what a chance!
With each little push, we shoot down fast,
Laughter erupts, snow flies, and we blast!

With every tumble, we giggle and roll,
Snowflakes tickle, and we lose control!
Dress warm, they said, in layers galore,
But half of it's melting by the time we hit the floor!

Mittens are soggy, and noses are red,
Who knew ice dungeons caused such dread?
We chase each other, like deer on the run,
Spinning and swirling, oh what fun!

At last, we collapse in a pile of snow,
Wiping our tears, hearts all aglow.
From ice to laughter, we find our stride,
In our little world, there's no need to hide!

Winter Wonderland Rush

Oh the thrill of racing down the hill,
With sleds and friends, we scream and thrill.
The snow flies up, a frosty delight,
We crash and we laugh, what a snowy sight!

A lopsided grin, we tumble and slide,
With flakes in our hair, we take it in stride.
Snowmen are laughing, their buttons askew,
As we speed past with a giggle or two.

Hot cocoa waits at the end of the day,
But first, let us swerve and spin our way.
It's a ballet of clumsiness, pure and absurd,
Each icy adventure, a line from the herd!

With cheeks a rosy and spirits so high,
We forge through the winter, just laughing, oh my!
As long as we're together, we'll revel and play,
In this sparkling land where we dream away!

Cold Cascades

The hill looms large, gleaming and bright,
With sleds we ascend, what a dizzying height!
A push and a whoosh, off we go in a flash,
Landing in snow with an ungraceful crash!

Jackets get snagged, pants soaked through,
But look at the fun; could this really be true?
Rolling in laughter, our faces aglow,
Eating snowflakes, our own winter show!

With flurries around us, we twist and we spin,
Who's winning the race? No one can win.
Chasing the jingle of joy in the chill,
We're crafting memories atop this winter hill!

As dusk settles in, we shuffle on home,
With mittens all soggy and hearts full of foam.
What tales we'll tell of our icy brigade,
In this blizzard of laughter, a friendship we made!

Frosty Descent

Wipe the fog off the goggles, it's time to race,
Each one of us eager to find our place.
With a sprint and a leap, we launch down the slope,
Giggling like children, we've caught winter's hope!

The bump on the hill sends us spinning around,
Like piñatas in snow, we're lost, then we're found.
A snowball flies past with astonishing speed,
But we shake off the chill, it's the laughter we need!

Those flips and those flops, what a grand sport!
A frosty adventure, the best kind of court.
With hats all askew, we march back for more,
Plotting new schemes as we burst through the door!

So here's to the season, to snowflakes and cheer,
To laughter and antics, winter's extra gear.
In this frosty descent, our spirits take flight,
With each push and each slip, everything feels right!

Milton Keynes UK
Ingram Content Group UK Ltd.
UKHW020816141124
451205UK00012B/610